Dog Overboard

Written by Lisa Thompson
Pictures by Craig Smith and Lew Keilar

Bones, the sea dog, was learning to barrel walk.

It was a new trick. He wasn't very good at it yet.

2

3

Bones was barrel walking the top deck when a giant wave hit the boat.

Bones and his barrel bounced off the ship.

They were thrown overboard into the sea.

"Dog overboard!" cried Captain Red Beard.

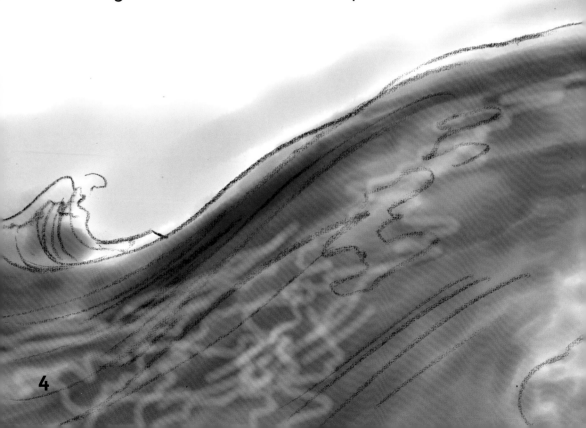

"Help! Help!" yelped Bones.

Lizzie, the first mate, tried to throw Bones a line.

It wasn't long enough.

The cook threw Bones a big pot, but it sank.

"Silly rotten pirates," said Fingers the parrot.

Bones was lost at sea. The waves grew bigger.
The waves tossed Bones about.

He climbed on top of the barrel. Bones surfed
the sea.

He drifted all through the night.

Bones was tired, cold, and hungry.

The next morning, Bones and his barrel washed up onto a small island.

Bones found food and water.

He made a hut out of sticks and leaves
and had a sleep.

Bones dreamed about sailing the seas
and finding treasure.

When Bones woke up, he had a plan.
He would make a lookout and a bonfire.

Bones searched the jungle and
the beach for wood.

He made a tall lookout and
a large pile of wood.

15

He stood in the lookout and searched the sea for ships.

He saw fish, dolphins, a whale, and lots of birds. He did not see a ship.

He waited day and night, night and day. While he waited he practiced his barrel-walking trick.

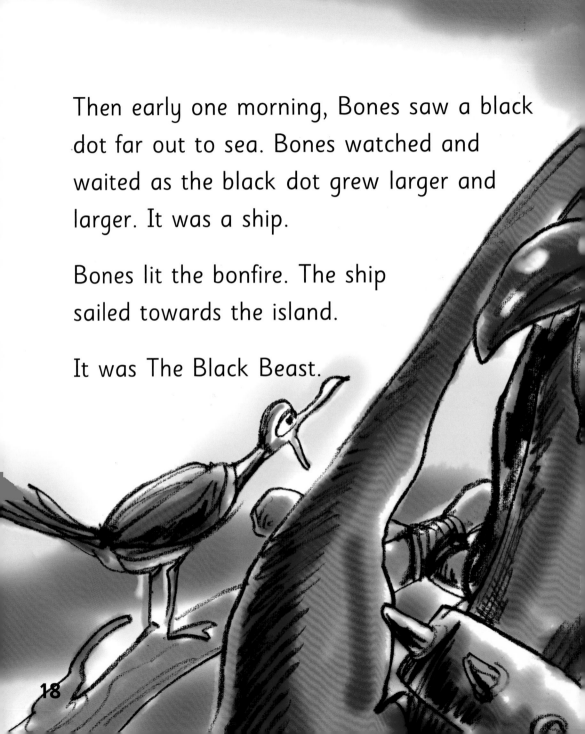

Then early one morning, Bones saw a black dot far out to sea. Bones watched and waited as the black dot grew larger and larger. It was a ship.

Bones lit the bonfire. The ship sailed towards the island.

It was The Black Beast.

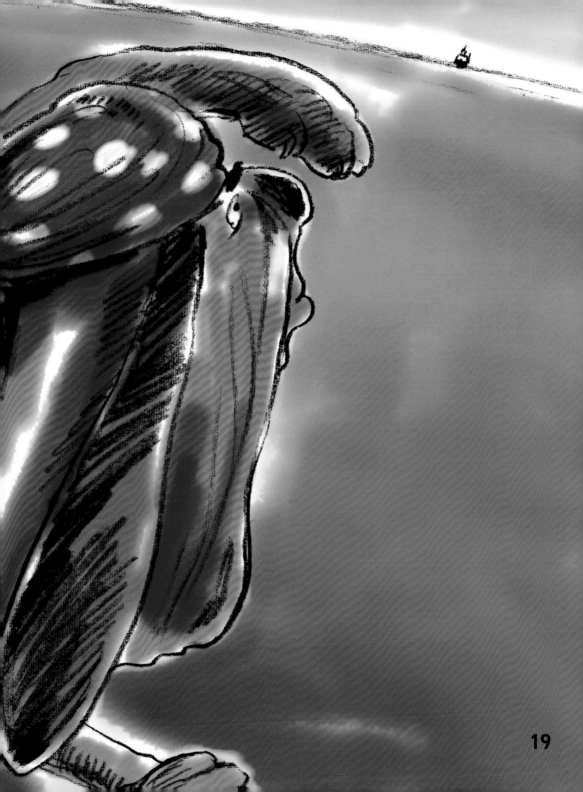

19

The crew of The Black Beast rowed to the beach.

"I've been waiting for you!" said Bones.

"We searched for you everywhere!" said Lizzie.

Bones was rescued.

"Climb aboard!" said Captain Red Beard. "We've got treasure to find."

"And I've got a new trick to show you," said Bones.